Facing Adversity
VICTORIOUSLY

30-DAY DAILY
DEVOTIONAL

Carolyn Coleman-Grady

TRILOGY
PROFESSIONAL PUBLISHING MEETS POWERFUL PROMOTION

A wholly owned subsidary of TBN

Manufactured in the United States of America
10 9 8 7 6 5 4 3 2 1
Library of Congress Cataloging-in-Publication Data is available.
ISBN: 978-1-63769-864-8
E-ISBN: 978-1-63769-865-5

DEDICATION

To my loving husband, Frederick M. Grady. You are the love of my life! Also, to my three sons: Vincent, Frederick Allen, and Brandon. To my parents, Allen and Lillian Carter, and to siblings, Kenneth, Cynthia, and Carmen.

ENDORSEMENT

Carolyn Coleman-Grady's *Facing Adversity Victoriously* is a powerful tell-all devotional people of faith can identify with.

Carolyn unapologetically shares personal and intimate details of her life. The author's unwavering faith in God triumphantly overcomes in the face of adversities.

The daily devotions are a treasure trove of wisdom, knowledge, and poignant scriptures. Carolyn places God's word in the center of her sorrow, igniting the peace of Christ in the lives of the chosen! A must-read.

—Allen Carter, Jr.
Father and author

TABLE OF CONTENTS

INTRODUCTION

There are certain circumstances in life that don't make sense. They can leave us feeling empty, misunderstood, broken, or even further from what we envisioned would be our lives.

There are so many dreams that become deferred and ghosts from the past that still haunt us, leaving the blanket of faith that we once wrapped around our hearts tattered and torn.

I know! I have been here many times within my life and have witnessed my mother there, crawling to find her way back to her own dreams and to the understanding of herself.

Her road was not paved with riches but with abuse, sickness, low self-esteem, and a loneliness that defined so many aspects of her life. Yet through all of the adversity, I witnessed her grow stronger, even when it may have felt like life was no longer worth fighting for. It was beautiful to see.

Her devotion and trust in God brought healing for her emotionally, physically, and spiritually. It inspired me because, in the face of adversity, we all ask, "How am I going to get through this?" At times it's easier to give up and give in, yet in seeing my mother persist, the answer became clear.

When I think about the definition of faith, at its core, it's a relationship, an agreement, or an alignment of the supernatural or spiritual with our lived experience.

Witnessing my mother move through her circumstances

with an openness to transform and be changed for the better, I realized that just like every relationship, faith takes work, time, commitment, and honesty. It takes a willingness to forgive and be forgiven. It takes a reflection of your journey thus far with eyes wide open in order to see the lessons that have been revealed to you.

Life will always include hardships and struggles. Yet, your devotion to your faith will provide a peace that goes beyond all understanding and a pathway to your healing that may not look exactly as you envisioned. It will fulfill everything that God knows you need. Faith with works is the key to your ability to "get through this."

I pray that through the daily work of *Facing Adversities Victoriously: 30-Day Daily Devotional*, written beautifully and transparently by my mother, you discover new life, new tools, and a newfound devotion to the love of God and love of self.

May this devotional help you to overcome every trial and tribulation with triumph and celebration. When circumstances bring about discouragement and a feeling of being stuck, may you find comfort and encouragement.

I pray that you rediscover who you are through your reignited relationship to faith. And once you're done, look back at your journey. Reread what you wrote and allow yourself to learn new lessons, see more opportunities for life, and share your growth with others. We're all looking for a way to face adversity victoriously.

—Vincent Coleman
Son and author

DAILY DEVOTIONAL: DAY 1

God, Where Are You?

Have you ever wondered if God really hears our cry? So often, we are surrounded by turmoil. Sometimes, it's difficult to see the hand of God at work in our lives. I remember when I was molested; it was a very difficult time for me. There were many days I felt alone, and it seemed that no one cared or believed me. I often wondered where God was and why He did not help me. Did I deserve it? Had I done something to invite this violation of my body, mind, and spirit? I gathered it was not my fault. And, I surely did not deserve it. How does one renew their mind and trust again? How do you love again? This act of violation against my body created trauma, a trauma that led to destructive, promiscuous behavior as I tried to reconnect and relearn two of the most important puzzle pieces of my life: love and trust. Looking back on this dark time in my life, I needed God more than anything, just as I need Him still today.

> As for God, his way is perfect: the word
> of the Lord is tried: he is a buckler to all
> those that trust in him.
>
> **Psalm 18:30 (KJV)**

Even in the midst of the violation against my body, I had to

ll

remind myself to trust in God and allow Him to renew my mind, to accept that God is my protector and that His desire is to embrace us with His love. Being embraced by His love brought about a forgiveness that led to my road of recovery, a road that I am still on, yet a road that has become smoother because I had aligned my faith in God with my desire to heal and be made whole again.

Genesis 34 (NKJV) talks about a young girl by the name of Dinah, the daughter of Jacob. She was raped by the prince of the region. This was devastating to Dinah and her family. I imagine that Dinah felt the sting of guilt and shame, though it was not her fault; *she* had been defiled. In my own violation, I felt defiled, guilty, ashamed, isolated, and broken. I believed that no one cared, not even God. So I placed God in a box, believing He would not save me from the torment that developed in my mind.

Sometimes, as a result of trauma, we put God in a box, limiting the power He has within our lives. I sure did. These limitations hindered me from calling out to Him in my most vulnerable state, yet, in Matthew 11:28-30 (KJV), God says:

> Come unto me all ye that labour and are heavy laden, and I will give you rest. Take my yoke upon you, and learn of me; for I am meek and lowly in heart: and ye shall find rest unto your souls. For my yoke is easy and my burden is light.

Have you ever experienced a heaviness that affected

your rest? I cannot count the numerous times I have cried out to God in a desperate time of my life. We try to fix our problems while forgetting how much God loves and adores us, how much He wants to lift us out of the pit of despair and establish our steps through restoration.

So the reflection for today is: *Where would you like God to make you whole?* This question may cause you discomfort or fear of not having an answer, and that's okay. Anytime we are challenged to face the thing that has contributed to our brokenness, struggle rises up as well. Yet, let's take the first steps to answer this question together.

Reflection

What does being made whole mean to you?

_____

_____

_____

_____

Where would you like God to make you whole?

_____

_____

_____

_____

What can God provide to help begin your journey towards wholeness? Write it down and ask Him for it, having faith that He will provide.

_____

_____

_____

_____

_____

Prayer

Lord, thank You for renewing our minds and restoring us through Your love. Thank You for moving through our lives, straightening out the crooked roads of guilt and shame, and providing us with a way of escape through your loving kindness and tender mercies. Your word says in Psalm 25:20 (KJV): "O keep my soul, and deliver me: let me not be ashamed, for I put my trust in thee." Lord, help us lean not to our own understanding and trust You more. In Jesus' name. Amen.

DAILY DEVOTIONAL: DAY 2

Leaning Not to Our Own Understanding

God promises if we trust in Him with all of our heart and lean not unto our own understanding, always acknowledging Him, that He'll direct our path (Proverbs 3:5-6, KJV). Our desire to do things on our own and, at times, out of selfish will can be a stronghold in our lives. What a mess we can easily become when fighting to be the director of our own show.

One afternoon, a friend and I went for a drive in my 1968 brown Cadillac. We were laughing, playing music loudly, enjoying being reckless, and having a good time. As I turned right onto 110th Street and Crenshaw Boulevard Street, I pushed the pedal to the metal, wanting to show off my Cadillac and laughing at all of the slow drivers that were around us, not caring at all about their safety; I wanted to show off in my car. All of a sudden, a driver sped up and stopped their car beside us. Boy, was she angry, yelling obscenities as she followed us, pulling up to the driver's side whenever she could to yell even more. My friend and I both became frightened and determined to do anything to get away from her. We drove faster and faster, yet she continued to speed up, committed to chasing us. I drove as fast as I could, swerving through narrowed residential streets. Families were playing outside, basketballs rolling into the street, yet none of this mattered: my friend and I needed to get away from this driver. By the grace of God, there were no accidents, and we finally escaped the wrath of this driver as she turned down another street, yet I know God was not happy with my pride and ego driving my decision to show off in my Cadillac, again with no care or concern for others. We never did that again, and, to this day, I am thankful for His protection even in the midst of my being driven by my own will.

God has created a wonderful brain inside of us, one that has the ability to process and make good decisions. Oftentimes, we do not. God never intended us to make bad decisions that affect our lives and the lives of others. My friend and I leaned to our own understanding and made a foolish decision that could have cost us our life. But God and praying parents! The word of God says this: "A man's heart deviseth his way: but the Lord directeth his steps" (Proverbs 16:9, KJV). The best decision in our case was to wait on the driver, and if we had to pass by, to do it with patience and safety, remembering the importance of doing the right thing.

God grants us wisdom when we ask for it. Leaning to our own understanding can lead us down uncomfortable paths.

The book of Genesis, in chapter 16, talks about Sarai, the wife of Abram. Sarai could not conceive a child, so she devised a plan in her own mind without consulting God. She told her husband, Abram, to sleep with an Egyptian slave named Hagar, who gave him a boy and named him Ishmael, a decision that created quite a mess within their family. Envy and jealousy visited them all, causing Sarai to want both the Egyptian slave and her baby exiled. Abram honored his wife's request and exiled Hagar, yet God always has a better plan for our lives, just as he did for Hagar and Sarai.

God wants us to trust Him and acknowledge Him in all our ways. It is then we see the move of God in our choices and decisions.

A great example of this is King Solomon, who did not ask for silver and gold but rather for wisdom and understanding to rule over the people; God heard his prayers, granting him a wise and understanding heart according to 1 Kings 3:12 (KJV). We see the difference when we lean into our own understanding rather than that of God: both actions received results; however, the better result is when we allow God to direct and establish our path.

Reflection

Identify a time in your life when you leaned into your own understanding.

_____

_____

_____

_____

How did God redirect you?

_____

_____

_____

_____

Prayer

Lord God, Your promises are sure. Help us understand that You have the best-laid plans for our lives. Thank You for always being there when we call. Your word says in Hebrews 12:2 (NKJV): "Looking unto Jesus the author and finisher of our faith, who for the joy that was set before Him endured the cross, despising the shame and has sat down at the right hand of the throne of God." Help us today to embrace the plans You have for our lives. In Jesus' name, we pray. Amen.

DAILY DEVOTIONAL: DAY 3

Dealing with Rejection

He came to that which was his own, but
his own did not receive him.

John 1:11 (KJV)

Have you ever stood in the mirror and asked yourself, "Who am I?" Many times we are finding something wrong with us—our hair, skin tone, our bodies—even, at times, wishing we looked like someone else. We start to create a system of questioning our self-worth and begin to believe no one else could possibly find us valuable. I experienced these feelings the first time during a high school tradition known as the Senior Kidnap.

Every year, the senior class hosts a breakfast at a local diner with upwards of ninety to a hundred seniors in attendance, all eagerly waiting to eat while hanging out in their pajamas. On the day of the Senior Kidnap, classmates would throw toilet paper all over the front yard as a sign to their families that your senior had been kidnapped and the festivities had begun. The night before the event, my mom came into my room and handed me some money. "Keep this with you; you may need it," she said, aware of this tradition and preparing me, me being unaware of the senior kidnapping that would occur. Yet, no one showed up for me. I felt awful, and I began to give in to the system of questioning my self-worth: *Was I not chosen because of my weight? I mean, who would want me in their car? Was I not special enough? Did my friends not actually care about me?* What a deal-breaker for my self-esteem! I felt left out and not ready to face everyone the next day at school. All the seniors that attended would be talking about how much fun they had. But not me.

Psalm 27:10 says, "When my father and my mother forsake me, then the Lord will take me up." My parents did not forsake me; in fact, they supported me. Yet, I felt that my friends had forsaken me, and those feelings bred a stronghold of rejection that I wasn't sure how to deal with, yet God, through the love of Jesus Christ, helped to cover that rejection with His love.

God's kind of love is unconditional. The love that endures forever.

Reflection

Write down three things that make you feel rejected.

_____

_____

_____

_____

In what areas of your life do you need to forgive yourself?

_____

_____

_____

_____

How are you allowing God to shower you with His acceptance?

_____

_____

_____

_____

Prayer

Father God, thank You for accepting me for who I am in Christ Jesus. Thank You for creating me in Your image. Because You are acquainted with rejection, I know that You understand my misunderstandings and that You will be there, reminding me that I am not alone when I am feeling at my lowest. Thank You for turning my ashes into beauty. In Jesus' name, I pray. Amen.

DAILY DEVOTIONAL: DAY 4

Whimpering in the Night

I lay there at night. A cry of distress, whimpering silently in the night. Who will come to my rescue? I'm restless, tossing, sleep-deprived. Who will come to my rescue? That's the way I felt when my first husband decided to leave. I was devastated. I believed my life was over. We had been married for five years, five years of confusion, love, fear, and disappointment, filled with verbal and physical abuse. And yet, I longed for him to stay. I was pregnant and did not want my future son to live in this world without a father. But as life would have it, what I did not want, happened.

He left.

With my back against the floor of a room in my parents' home, I cried for days, erecting a wall of grief and sadness; completely desolate, my life felt shattered.

One morning, my dad knocked on the door, entered the room, and said: "Daughter, how long will you cry about this?" Then he walked out of the room. I was left there to consider my options. I could continue in my grief and self-pity or get up and follow life again. So, with trepidation and a hint of hesitancy, I decided to pick up my body and walk.

When I look back, it reminds me that life is not always fun, exciting, or easy. Actually, Christ never said life would be easy. But He did say in Psalm 30:5 (KJV): "For his anger endureth but a moment; In his favor is life: weeping may endure for a night, but joy cometh in the morning." God knows what we need: sometimes it is an encouraging word from someone like my dad or a Psalm from the word of God to lead us back to the life we've been promised through Christ Jesus.

> For God so loved the world, that he gave his only begotten Son, that whosoever believeth in him should not perish, but have everlasting life.
>
> **John 3:16 (KJV)**

Reflection

Let's meditate on Psalm 30:5 together again.

> For his anger endureth but a moment; In his favor is life:
> Weeping may endure for a night, but joy cometh in the morning.

Think about a time when you wept during the night, yet when morning came, you felt the joy of the Lord enter your heart.

Take a few minutes to write down how God has comforted you during your time of sorrow.

_____

_____

Day 4

_____

_____

_____

_____

_____

_____

Prayer

Lord, thank You for helping us through difficult times in our lives. It is comforting knowing that You are always with us even through tough times. When I feel weak, You make me strong. Thank You for Your loving concern for each of us. In Jesus' name, I pray. Amen.

DAILY DEVOTIONAL:
DAY 5

Aha! Look at Them! I Knew They Would Fall

In 2020, the world experienced a global pandemic that changed our entire understanding of both life and death. So many families experienced loss, including that of my own, losing two relatives to COVID-19. Those deaths were difficult to process, especially that we were not able to attend the celebrations of their lives due to the severity of the pandemic. On the day of their home-going, while trying to process their deaths and seemingly trapped by the state of the world, it felt as if everything was falling apart around me. I was agitated and tearful. I even lashed out at my husband. I could not find a way to escape the grips of despair. I knew God had the answers, and yet I felt I could not reach Him. But then, He sent his Holy Spirit to remind me of His sovereignty and how much Jesus loves me. It is always comforting to know that God will answer us in times of trouble when we remember that He wants us to lay down our burdens before Him. Psalm 30:2 (KJV) says: "O Lord my God, I cried unto thee and thou hast healed me." I needed healing of the mind, heart, and soul, a reminder that He was still in control and that His love could bring about a peace that surpasses all understanding.

I Will extol thee, O Lord; for thou hast
lifted me up, and hast not made my foes
to rejoice over me.

Psalm 30:1 (KJV)

King David cried out to the Lord in his time of trouble
and transgressions. David believed that God would vindicate
him, and God rejoiced in his victories, just as God does
today. He rejoices in all of our victories.

We must decide that when life challenges us, we will
not hide from God and remember that His promises are
unchanging. In the face of adversity, we can wait on the
Lord, and He will provide what we need. In times of despair,
we must remember to "sing unto the Lord, O ye saints of
his, and give thanks at the remembrance of his holy name"
(Psalm 30:4, KJV).

Reflection

Take a moment to reflect on a challenging day that caused
your mind to become weary. Reflect on God's promises to
us as His children and write down what you needed from
God in that moment. Then write down how God may
have comforted you in that moment or how God may be
comforting you now.

_____

_____

_____

Prayer

Lord, thank You for helping me when I am weary. I trust in Your comfort and rely on Your saving grace. You are my strength and my strong tower. In Jesus' name, I pray. Amen.

DAILY DEVOTIONAL: DAY 6

When Illness, Sickness, and Disease Knock at Your Door

But He was wounded for our transgressions, He was bruised for our iniquities; The chastisement for our peace, was upon Him and by His stripes we are healed.

Isaiah 53:5 (NKJV)

Battling cancer in 2015 nearly wiped out my spirit. I cried, I felt alone, I was angry and confused. I did not understand. I believed I was a good person; I helped as many as I could and was encouraging to others. Yet, I had these burning questions that would not go away: *Why Lord? Why cancer?*

When I received the diagnosis, I began to reflect on the life that I had lived so far and all of the things that my life could have been; I thought this would be the end. My day began with a scheduled routine check-up. My gynecologist performed a wellness check of my uterus; she collected tissue specimens, and I went on about my day. During my follow-up visit, she mentioned that she did not check my cervix during my last visit. I responded, "It's okay; you did not find anything in the uterus." She was persistent and said, "No, they are different, and we had better check. Follow up with me in one week." The front desk arranged a visit for one week. I left and drove back to work. The following week, I arrived for my scheduled appointment, and the nursing staff prepared me for the check-up. My doctor entered the room and began to remind me of how important it is to stay healthy. I admit I tuned out, as this is a common protocol within the industry. As she began her examination, I heard her say, "Oh, what is this?" which initiated a sense of panic within my body. I responded, "What is what? What do you mean?" She continued, "I see something…it looks like a purse with a handle." My panic widened as the fear of the unknown began to grow. She began to twist; she twisted and twisted, and I felt so much pain. Removing the tissue from my body, she brought it up to my eyesight, and there it was, a growth that resembled a purse with straps. Off to the lab that little piece of tissue went.

Before I left, the doctor turned to me and said, "You know, Carolyn, I was sent here to save you?" I smiled and walked out of the office and thought no more about it.

Five days later, she called, mentioning that she'd like to see me in the office. I was so busy at work that there was no time to return to her office again. I requested that she just tell me over the phone.

"Are you sitting down?" she asked.

"No!" I responded.

"Well, if you can sit down, I have something to tell you,"

"Doctor, just tell me!"

"You have *cancer,* and I have already arranged an appointment for you with one of the best surgeries in this area; he will see you on Monday. It is very important that you follow up."

I went back to my work. I wasn't able to process this news quite yet. When I arrived home, I shared the news with my husband, and he became tearful. I found myself consoling him. But soon after my consoling, he began consoling me. No one wants to hear the word "cancer." All I can remember through my tears was hearing my husband say, "Honey, it is going to be alright, just fine." And somehow, I believed him.

I followed up with the surgeon. He was pretty; as a matter of fact, his bedside manner was not very good. But he was the best surgeon for women's gynecological issues in the area. So, I ignored his behavior and focused on his knowledge and skills. We discussed options, and his front office scheduled a total hysterectomy. Everything inside would be removed. Sounds simple, right? That night all the information started sinking in; I was frantic, emotional, and very afraid, seemingly losing grip of myself. I began to yell, travailing; my poor husband did not know what to do, so he sat there, holding my hand. The phone rang; my sisters were calling. I picked up; they both heard the distress in my voice and rushed right over. It seemed as if they just appeared out of nowhere. They comforted me and reminded me how good God is and that everything will be fine. All of my tears, fears, concerns, anger, confusion, and disappointment combined into a migraine. I somehow found the energy to finally fall asleep and was able to get rest.

The next evening, I called a meeting with my family. We met at my youngest sister's home and phoned my brother, who lives in Dallas, Texas.

"Family. I have cancer, and my surgery is scheduled ten days from now."

Of course, the room went silent; then, my three sons began to cry. My nephew came right over and hugged me with tears. I tried to remain strong, reminding them that I was not dead, yet the fear of this cancer leading to death permeated the room, and honestly, my subconscious because I was afraid of it as well.

On the day of surgery, I was very nervous. I had been told what to expect, and I knew the surgery would be a robotic-assisted laparoscopic hysterectomy; in other words, a surgery completed by a remote surgeon controlling a robotic arm. When I entered the room, that same panic that found its way into my body when I was first diagnosed found home in me again. In the corner was a tall white and black robot, reminiscent of a huge transformer. There I lay on the hospital bed, yelling over and over, "What is that over there?" That was the last moment I can recall as the anesthesiologist put me to sleep quickly.

When I awoke, I was informed that the cancer had been removed, encapsulated within the area where the tissue that resembled a purse had been. It was sent to the lab, and the results returned Stage 1 uterine cancer. No chemotherapy or radiation needed.

I remember the gynecologist saying, "I am here to save you." God sent an angel to work through her. He had already set everything in motion. Now, I am seven years cancer-free. I know that everyone's story is different. This is my story. However, what is the same is the healing hand of God and His constant love and comfort.

Jesus said, in John 14:18 (KJV): "I will not leave you comfortless: I will come to you." I believe He came to me that day to give me a touch of healing and comfort.

Reflection

How has God comforted you in time of need? Write down a few times where you have experienced His love and healing hand.

_____

_____

_____

_____

_____

_____

_____

_____

Prayer

Lord, thank You for standing at the door of illness and walking with me through the challenges of sickness and disease. You carried all our infirmities on the cross, and we were healed. I choose today to trust in Your healing hand, knowing assuredly that You will never leave or forsake me. I receive your loving, tender care today. In Jesus' name. Amen.

DAILY DEVOTIONAL: DAY 7

The Cowardly Lion

For I know the thoughts that I think toward you, saith the Lord, thoughts of peace, and not of evil, to give you an expected end. Jesus loves us, and he wants us to have courage.

Jeremiah 29:11 (KJV)

Have you ever felt like a cowardly lion? I sure have. Sometimes it is hard to find courage; the courage to love, sing, live alone, enter into a relationship, or allow yourself to heal, just to name a few. How do you find courage? If we do not have courage, then we walk in doubt and fear. I remember walking on the stage of Big Beautiful Women (BBW), a small modeling group contest, which I had been entered into by a company that I was referred to by a close friend. Those selected would model clothing that women of larger frames could wear and feel beautiful in. Being a model was a childhood dream come true, as I often pretended to walk a runway in my private time locked in my bedroom and dreamed of owning the runway. I started practicing my runway walk again over and over and over, down to the minute the contest was scheduled to begin. I peered out into the audience from the backstage; the place was filled with people waiting with anticipation. As each name of a contestant was called, I could feel my excitement and nervousness the closer it got to my turn. Name after name was called, and, finally, it was my time to walk onto the stage and answer a preselected question—questions that were randomly selected and ones we were not given privy to. So my answer would have to be spontaneous and hopefully filled with truth. My answer would need to be powerful and sincere, something that would turn the heads of the audience and inspire the hearts of the judges.

I made my way forward, the host looking at me, placing the microphone to their lips, asking, "Why do you think you should be the next BBW winner?" The moment my brain processed the question, my mouth spoke words that made me feel embarrassed and immature. The room became silent: everyone's eyes were on me, and I could see their disgust. One of the judges put her head down. Their foreheads held signs that said "loser" and "failure." I felt horrible. I didn't have the courage to say thank you to the host or the trainer. I disappeared into the shadows of the crowds. At that moment, I believed God was disappointed in me too. I knew my chances of winning were zero. Devastated by these events, I didn't have and couldn't find the courage to return for the next model training. Whatever courage I had that helped me walk up those flights of stairs in three-inch heels flew right out the window. I embraced defeat. Even if modeling were a part of my future, I quit and gave up the journey. I didn't find the courage to stand before anyone else. My courage and trust in myself had disappeared.

Have you ever felt like giving up and shutting the shades of your future? In Matthew 14:27 (KJV), Jesus encourages us all: "But straightway Jesus spoke unto them, saying, Be of good cheer; it is I; be not afraid." In other words, immediately take courage to devour fear and discouragement. Take courage when you need to align your journey with the will of God. When I think of courage, I am reminded of Joshua of the Bible. Joshua was chosen and appointed by God before Moses' death to be Israel's leader. Can you imagine a charge like this? Leading people into the promised land, Joshua loved and served the Lord until his death. In fact, he said publicly, "Choose for yourselves, this day whom you will serve, […] but as for me and my household, we will serve the Lord" (Joshua 24:15, NIV). Joshua had the courage to proclaim God before the people. God said to Joshua in Joshua 1:7-9 (NIV):

> Be strong and very courageous. Be careful to obey all the laws my servant Moses gave you; do not turn from it to the right or to the left, that you may be successful wherever you go. Keep this Book of the Law always on your lips; meditate on it day and night, so that you may be careful to do everything written in it. Then you will be prosperous and successful. Have I not commanded you? Be strong and courageous. Do not be afraid; do not be discouraged, for the Lord your God will be with you wherever you go.

I was afraid before walking up the stairs, speaking negative words to myself before the question was asked. I told myself I could never be a model, and it hindered my success. Joshua also experienced fear, yet he decided to trust God and believe that he would not be alone. God would be with him through his charge.

He knew that God would never leave him or forsake him. Joshua had to depend on God without turning to the left or the right. His courage and strength came from God. When we draw from other sources, including relying on our own strength, we tend to fall. But, with God, all things are possible if we only believe. Trusting God with the plans for our lives is key. It doesn't mean we will not make bad decisions, but it means we can access the courage to make a choice, and when we examine ourselves and trust God, as Joshua did, we will be successful and prosperous.

Reflection

What experience in your life has caused you to abandon courage?

_____

_____

_____

_____

_____

_____

_____

Now reflect on how God restored your courage. Write down a few words that acknowledge your courage, then find a scripture that helps you walk courageously.

_____

_____

_____

_____

_____

_____

_____

Prayer

Dear Lord, You alone give us the courage to run this race with grace, peace, and strength. Teach us Thy ways, oh Lord, so our hearts and minds will not faint, yet operate in the courage and support that Your word promises us. Thank You, Lord, for reminding us to have courage, which only comes from You. It is Your strength that helps us run this race with grace. When we become afraid, we know that Your love will see us through tough times. Thank You for wisdom to know that You are always there to help have courage. In Jesus' name. Amen.

DAILY DEVOTIONAL: DAY 8

Watching Your Finances Fly Out the Window

There is treasure to be desired and oil in the dwelling of the wise; but a foolish man spendeth it up.

Proverbs 21:20 (KJV)

In 2013, my husband and I experienced so many financial disasters that they seemed never-ending. One pitfall after another. We both worked and made a decent income, but neither of us was being responsible when it came to handling our household finances. One example of our negligence included us never opening mail: all mail was thrown on a small table in the living room, and it began to pile up. We would always say, "Let's take care of it another day." Little did we know that that willing negligence was creating a deeper hole for us to climb out of. We consistently found ourselves asking where was all the money going.

One morning I received a call from our landlord. He was calling to inform me that my husband had been late on the rent, and we were $5,000 behind. My eyes grew bigger than a lemon. With my voice shaking due to my disbelief, I asked the landlord to repeat what he said: "Your husband has been trying to pay the rent, I like him very much, but you are now $5,000 behind." I could not believe what I was hearing;

not only weren't he and I not opening mail, but we weren't communicating either. I apologized and asked if he could give us a few days. He agreed.

When my family arrived home, we had an emergency meeting. The details of our financial mess were shared, and we agreed to borrow the money from a relative. I made the call, explained the issue, and asked for a $5,000 loan. My relative agreed and drew up the loan papers. We were relieved, yet the recognition of the mess that we had made was overwhelming. We had allowed our negligence to remove both God and our responsibility from our own finances, yet, thankfully, He had provided us a way out, even in the midst of our mess.

Once we surrendered our finances to God, He began to show us the importance of stewardship, our finances, talents, time, and resources. It was an important lesson reminding us that if one of these areas is affected, all of these areas can potentially suffer.

"Let no debt remain outstanding except the continuing debt to love one another" (Romans 13:8, NIV). This scripture speaks volumes to me. My husband and I had great incomes, but what did it profit us if we did not love to steward what God had given us? Luke 14:28 (KJV) says this: "For which of you intend to build a tower, sitteth not down first, and counter the cost, whether he have [sufficient] to finish it?" We had in our mind that the well would never go dry. And it did. When we decided to surrender our full life to God, He began to train us and direct all areas of our lives. We decided together it was time to be obedient to what God wanted us to do in the area of finances. The loan was paid in full.

Reflection

> And God is able to make all grace abound toward you; that ye, always having all sufficiency in all things, may abound to every good work.
>
> **2 Corinthians 9:8 (KJV)**

Are you willing to surrender your finances to God and allow Him to teach you how to become a better financial steward? Write down ways you have rejected God's intervening in your finances. Be honest about it.

Based upon His word, how would you like to see God intervene on your behalf in the area of your finances?

_____

_____

_____

_____

_____

_____

_____

_____

_____

_____

_____

_____

Prayer

Lord, teach us Thy ways so that we may not stumble in the area of financial stewardship. Forgive us when we squander and spend our money foolishly. And Lord, forgive us for misusing the gifts, talents, and resources that You have provided for our wellbeing and our sustenance to glorify You. Help us see stewardship from Your eyes. We surrender and trust Your will in our finances. Thank You, Lord, for what You have entrusted us with. In Jesus' name. Amen.

DAILY DEVOTIONAL: DAY 9

Does God Really Hear Our Prayers?

While sitting in my living room, I'm reflecting on my prayer life, and I am questioning the effectiveness of my prayers.

> Rejoice always, pray without ceasing, in everything give thanks; for this is the will of God in Christ Jesus for you.
> **1 Thessalonians 5:16-18 (NKJV)**

In the New Testament, Jesus taught His disciples how to pray. Just as He has instructed them, through His word, He has also instructed us. In Matthew 6:9-13 (KJV), Jesus instructs us to pray as follows:

> Our Father which art in heaven, Hallowed be thy name. Thy kingdom come, Thy will be done in earth, as it is in heaven. Give us this day our daily bread. And forgive us our debts, as we forgive our debtors. And lead us not into temptation, but deliver us from evil; For thine is the kingdom, and the power, and the glory, for ever. Amen.

Many of us are familiar with the Lord's Prayer, and yet,

at times, it may feel ineffective. The toughest challenge in prayer is praying the will of God. Our Father in heaven is so awesome. He knows our thoughts and the conditions of our hearts.

One day, as I was preparing lunch for my husband, *I heard the Lord say, "Come and communion with me."* Of course, my flesh wanted not to sit at the table, but my spirit was willing to sit and connect with God. I heard the Lord say, "Daughter, why are you fretting?" Reflecting on this word from God, I confessed that I felt my prayers were ineffective. I have seen prayers answered in my life, but an overwhelming feeling brought doubt. The Lord reminded me of this, "Confess your faults one to another, and pray one for another, that ye may be healed. The effectual fervent prayer of the righteous prayer availeth much" (James 5:16, KJV). He also reminded me that He will direct my path, and the Holy Spirit will reveal to me what I ought to pray for. This was a reminder that our Father is always on time. When doubt and uncertainty speak to us, our God reminds us who we are in Him. The Bible says: "Pray without ceasing" (1 Thessalonians 5:17, KJV). God hears our prayers. We must believe by faith that He will answer. We must walk in what we expect, believe we have received. The promises of God are yes and amen.

I will rejoice in the Lord's loving kindness. Amen.

Reflections

Write down what you believe is hindering your prayer life.

_____

_____

_____

_____

How has God reset your thinking in the area of prayer?

_____

_____

_____

_____

How are you building a closer relationship with God?

_____

_____

_____

_____

Prayer

Lord, help us to go deeper in our relationship with You. We desire to spend more time in Your presence, but oftentimes, we feel unworthy. Help us to turn to You through prayer. We desire to communicate and build up our most holy faith through our prayer and reading Your word. Teach us to wait on You, Lord. Your plans for our lives are bigger than we could ever imagine. We desire a closer, intimate walk with You, Lord. We acknowledge You in all our ways so that You will direct our path. Lord, teach us how to pray for Your will in our lives. In Jesus' name. Amen.

DAILY DEVOTIONAL: DAY 10

You Always Start Something!

Have you ever encountered an argument that was started by someone else? I was having a pretty good day: no issues, smooth sailing. In fact, it was a day of relaxing and enjoying the moments. My husband arrived home from a long day of work, and he was tired. After taking a shower and changing his clothing, he walked down the stairs, had a seat, and began sharing how his workday had gone.

Things were going along fine; until a movie came on that involved betrayal, mistrust, infidelity, and murder. My husband made a comment on the protagonist of the film, saying, "I don't know why she became so angry; he paid her off with ten million dollars to cover all the money he had used during their marriage, paid off her mother's home, and she is still upset with him. She asked for divorce. Now that he is with someone else and has made it big with the invention he worked so hard to perfect, she is upset. I don't get it." Well, we surely did not agree on the events of this couple's relationship.

From my perspective, here you have a couple that was married, with the wife working two jobs while the husband refused to work, wanting to concentrate on his project, perfecting a new type of battery which he believed would make him successful. He came into the marriage without a job, subsequently without any monetary contribution to provide for his family. He watched his wife add a third job just to keep them afloat and still did not suggest even part-time work as he worked on his invention. She, on the other hand, had a college degree and inherited a beautiful home plus $350,000 from her mother. To ensure that her husband continued working on his invention, she agreed he could use some of the money. Well, all the money but $1,000 was used. Their lights were turned off; they did not have much food to eat, all again, while his wife worked three jobs. Finally, a potential investor contacted him because his ex-girlfriend, who worked for a firm, heard about his invention. She was impressed enough to introduce him to her bosses. They loved his invention and offered him $100,000; he was so offended at the offer, he became angry and walked out of their office. As the young lady followed and called after him, he said, "How dare they offer me that little money so they can make tons of money off my invention? No, thank you," and he left. Well, the wife and sisters decided it was time for him to leave. Thus a request for divorce was presented to him by the wife. When the investor included a percentage of each battery sold, he accepted the offer. Of course, when he took the offer, he got engaged to his ex-girlfriend. When the wife heard about it, she wanted him back. That didn't happen and hardened her heart.

My husband and I discussed the movie at length; we weren't on the same page. He said the money she received covered the losses they experienced during the marriage. In my attempt to explain, I said, "Money never replaces a broken and contrite heart," which led us to a deeper argument and hurtful words.

My husband came to me for a hug. Well, stubborn me, said, "No, I don't want to." He continued to edge me on by the soft tone of his voice and the call of my name. I accepted his hug and remembered how much we truly loved one another. We apologized for the ugly things we said. It was forgiveness that reconciled and caused us to see our loving union through the heart of God.

God does not expect us to be perfect, but He does expect us to love, understand and be concerned about one another. And in that concern, we find love. God is love, so we must demonstrate love to one another. We must also allow Him to renew our minds through that love, to be open to change and transformation.

> Be gentle and ready to forgive; never hold grudges. Remember, the Lord forgave you, so you must forgive others.
> **Colossians 3:13 (TLB)**

Reflection

Think of a situation in your relationship that caused you to lose sight of one another's love. How did or has that bitterness affected your relationship with a spouse, family, friend, or even the church?

_____

_____

_____

_____

If you experienced anger, how will you allow yourself to meet God there and place it into His hands? How will you allow God to change, transform and renew your mind?

_____

_____

_____

_____

Prayer

Dear Lord, when I am weak, You help me to be strong. I confess that I struggle with anger and bitterness. There are triggers that blind me from sharing Your love with others I come in contact with. Teach me to love like You; Your love is unconditional. Teach me to forgive others quickly as You have forgiven me. Thank You for Your unmerited love towards me. In Jesus' name, I pray. Amen.

DAILY DEVOTIONAL: DAY 11

So Many Doors

Have you ever experienced a time in your life where the doors of opportunity seemed to open and close at the same time? Or, perhaps, many doors are opened, but they all lead to destruction? I know some doors opened in my life that led me the wrong way, yet, because of my parents and friends constantly praying for me, God spared me yet again.

Imagine for a moment walking down a hallway: all of the walls are white, but there are many doors on each side, some with names and others without. The doors with no name swing open as to invite you in. But straight ahead of you is one door that says "Project Operation." There is a hesitancy within you as you approach this door, but you walk forward, making your way towards it. First door on the left—sexual sin. Second door on the left—gambling and drinking. Next door—a kitchen with a female cooking food and two unknown people in the background. A fourth door where violence was taking place, with women fighting and harming one another, opens to the outside. Another door, a man working at the computer looks up and smiles. And as you notice these doors, the "Project Operation" door seems so unreachable. You are pulled to the door of immoral acts as your flesh is craving that door, but something continues to drive you forward. You say, "I can make it on my own," so the gambling and dishonest dealings door looks like a great, quick get-rich door. You try to go in, but something is pulling and tugging you back. You are five feet in front of the door that says "Project Operations," and a voice says this: "You aren't good enough to go in that door; nothing is there for you. With your limited knowledge and skills, you will get eaten up." You begin to slow down, and then what appears to be a brush of wind thrushes you forward to the door. As you are moved closer to the entrance of this door, you begin to question whether you should enter. It seems to welcome you, but you stand in front of it and do not move. The question becomes, whose voice are you listening to? Is this the voice of reason, the one who Jesus is? Is this the door that the Lord has set before you?

Jesus said in John 10:9 (KJV): "I am the door: by me if any man enters in, he shall be saved, and shall go in and out, and find pasture." In Revelation 3:8 (KJV): "I know thy works: behold, I have set before thee an open door, and no man can shut it: for thou has a little strength, and hast kept my word, and has not denied my name." God has predestined our lives and wants the best for us. He shall direct our paths, even when we are unsure of which door we are to enter and which door we are to keep closed.

Reflection

What door are you standing in right now? Are they doors which gratify pleasures of the flesh? God wants us to keep His name and not deny Him. Are you willing to walk through the open door that God has set before you? Write down how God has opened door after door for you and reflect on the blessings He has granted you.

_____

_____

_____

_____

Prayer

Lord, I thank You for opening doors that no man can shut. You have blessed me beyond measure. Forgive me for walking into doors that were directed by my flesh. I pray that You grant me the wisdom and understanding that only comes from You so that I may walk by faith into the doors that You have set for me. I am grateful for all of the opportunities given to me by You. In Jesus' name, I pray. Amen.

DAILY DEVOTIONAL: DAY 12

Bye For Now

As a parent, one challenge we face is watching our children fly the coop. Watching our children grow up and leave is the desire of most parents, but it is not easy watching them go. My husband and I have three sons, each of them exiting the nest at various ages. Neither of them left due to conflicts: two left for college, and the eldest was ready to find his own apartment. It was difficult each time one of them left. And if they had to return home, it became difficult to experience their departure over again.

The actual day our children left was very hard for me. I think my husband handled it better than I, or at least he appeared to. The next day, I actually cooked breakfast as if our boys still lived at home. When my husband and I shopped for food, we still shopped for five people instead of two. We soon got past this part and developed menu planning to help us shop efficiently, a strategy my mom taught my siblings and me many years ago. I was challenged for the first month without our sons. I texted, called, and sent emails. They were so kind and understanding; none of them made me feel as if I was a bother, though I felt like a bother, even knowing that they did not feel that way. Their leaving began a new journey of letting go and learning who I was again.

Months began to pass, and my husband and I began to

learn about ourselves again. We started focusing on things we loved to do, like going for a drive, watching a good movie, attending comedy shows, and going out to dinner every once and a while. We learned to love one another again. Sometimes, when our children are home, we can lose sight of who we are. Now that all our boys are gone, my husband and I have resurrected from the times we laid dormant to ensure our sons were equipped to meet the challenges of the world.

> Train up a child in the way he should go, and when he is old he will not depart from it.
>
> **Proverbs 22:6 (NKJV)**

As parents, it is very important to instill positive affirmations and the word of God into your children so, when they depart, it remains rooted. It does not mean they won't fall short of God's glory or our expectations; they will as we do and have. But instilling these qualities will carry them a long way. Qualities like love, honesty, faithfulness, integrity, loyalty, and commitment. Teaching our children to be observant of the company they keep, staying away from anything that breeds hate and supports personal detriment.

We should pray for our children that they remain rooted in the things of God. What keeps my husband and me focused? We have found joy in our children's dreams and happiness. Knowing that God, through His son Jesus, will watch over them wherever they may go. Their journey is set, and Jesus will never leave them or forsake them. We pray that our sons will be of good courage and hold fast to that which is good. Finally, we have decided not to expect our children to live our lives but for them to live the life God has set up for them.

Reflection

How has God helped you work through your journey of releasing your child or children, whether biological or spiritual? How has God brought you comfort when you had feelings of loneliness and fear for your child or children living on their own? Write down your thoughts below.

_____

_____

_____

_____

Prayer

Lord, show us how to accept our children's transition to adulthood. Teach us to let go with grace. Our children belong to You, Lord, so we trust the guidance and instructions You have for them. Thank You, Lord, for entrusting Your children to us. Wash their minds with Your word, comfort them when they are afraid, and strengthen them when they are weak. You are the God of abundance; I pray that each child is equipped and prepared through Your wisdom. You said in your word, "Listen as wisdom calls out! Hear as understanding raises her voice! She stands on the hilltops and at the crossroads" (Proverbs 8:1-2, NLT). I pray that our children be of good courage, hold fast to that which is good, and above all, love and serve You, Lord. In Jesus' name. Amen.

DAILY DEVOTIONAL: DAY 13

Chaos Everywhere

Two thousand twenty, a year of vision: this is what everyone called it. The world seemed to be united. People planned new businesses and developed witty inventions. Babies were born, marriages were planned—life seemed to be pressing forward. Yet, little did we know that a pandemic known as the coronavirus/COVID-19 would take our world and each of our lives by storm. The amount of loss experienced in 2020 into 2021 was overwhelming; death had hit record numbers. The world's economic system broke, and tension was everywhere. It appeared as if there was no way to escape. I kept finding myself asking, how do you navigate in a world of chaos?

In March of 2020, our lives were locked down. Stay home mandates and safety protocols were issued all over the globe; everyone must wear a mask, wash our hands, and practice social distance. In addition to this chaos, racial injustice resurfaced and resurrected bigotry and hatred, seemingly eradicating the compassion we should have for each other. We witnessed violence of the worse kind. Everyone was thrust into a whirlwind. Life as we knew it would never be the same. The pandemic has stifled what we believed was normal.

In uncertain times we must not lean to our understanding

but listen to the direction and instructions of God. God is the same yesterday, today, and forever (Hebrews 13:8). In the midst of chaos, God sends order and His peace. The question becomes, are you willing to embrace the peace of God and allow Him to direct your path even in the face of adversity?

> And the peace of God, which surpasses
> all understanding, will guard your hearts
> and your minds through Christ Jesus.
> **Philippians 4:7 (NKJV)**

We must maintain hope and faith in God during the storms of life, for He has promised that He will help us keep peace. We must guard our hearts and minds and continue to advance the kingdom of God even through chaotic times. When we are thrust into a chaotic state without a cause, stand firm on the word of God, and rejoice in him always, knowing steadfastly that with God all things are possible. It is possible to get through this pandemic, restore families, embrace peace, and love one another. Philippians 4:13 (NKJV) says: "I can do all things through Christ who strengthens me." God's will is that we stay strong and do not lose heart.

Reflection

How do you handle unexpected chaos in your life? How have you stood on the word of God when life is falling apart? Below, list a few times where you struggled to maintain your faith in God and also reflect on how God reminded you of His peace during those times.

_____

_____

_____

_____

_____

_____

_____

_____

Prayer

Father God, Your presence, oh Lord, is where I find peace. Thank You for knowing my name and loving me eternally. I can always count on Your grace and mercy. Thank You for standing with me in times of trouble, even when I believe You are too far to reach. Thank You for Your order, guidance, and instruction. Your love has kept me through the times of uncertainty, and for that, I give You glory and praise. In Jesus' name. Amen.

DAILY DEVOTIONAL: DAY 14

When You Feel Like Martha

It was a Saturday morning, and my husband and I decided we would barbecue together on the weekend. My husband asked me to text him the items we needed. As he did the grocery shopping, I began organizing the kitchen in preparation for the food he would bring home. While cleaning the kitchen, I noticed multiple items were out of place, oil from his previous cooking day was on the cabinet, and bottles of condiments were not closed completely. Things were out of order. In other words, the kitchen was not organized in the way *I* liked it. Even the lemon juice top was loose, dripping small amounts into the refrigerator. I could feel myself becoming irritated, entertaining those frustrating thoughts that rushed inside my brain. The more I entertained them, the more my mindset changed from joy and excitement to anger. I was not happy nor looking forward to our planned barbecue any longer. Of course, when he returned, I let him have it. I babbled so long about cooking, cleaning, and organizing that it changed the mood of the day and soured any sweetness.

My anger and frustration reminded me of the story of Martha, Mary's sister. In Luke 10:39-42 (NKJV), the story of Jesus and others arriving at the home of Mary and Martha is told, and, like we do today, Martha wanted to prepare a meal for their guest. Mary, on the other hand, was not concerned with what meal would be prepared. She wanted to hear the ministry of Jesus, so she sat at His feet. Martha, like me, became irritated and felt no one was concerned as she was providing a meal for Jesus as their guest. Martha, upset, came to Jesus and said, "Lord, doesn't it seem unfair to you that my sister just sits here while I do all the work? Tell her to come and help me." But the Lord said to her, "My dear Martha, you are worried and upset over all these details. There is only one thing worth being concerned about. Mary has discovered it, and it will not be taken away from her." Recalling this story in the moment of my frustration and anger reminded me of what was important: for my husband and me to enjoy this quality time together and to focus on the moments that bring joy and happiness. Paying attention to detail in everything can cause us to miss creating fun times in our lives. As Jesus has abundant grace for us, we should have abundant grace with one another.

Reflections

What is causing your anxiety, anger, or frustration today? Write them down below.

_____

_____

_____

_____

Reflecting on your list above, write down below how Jesus can help you find peace and focus in the areas of your life where anxiety, anger, and frustration are alive and well.

_____

_____

_____

_____

_____

_____

_____

Prayer

Lord, help me with my anxious feelings. You said in Philippians 4:6-7 (KJV):

> Be careful for nothing; but in every thing by prayer and supplication with thanksgiving let your request be made known unto God. And the peace of God, which passeth all understanding, shall keep your hearts and minds through Christ Jesus.

Thank You, Lord, for keeping my mind from anxious thoughts. Help me with showing grace to others. In Jesus' name. Amen.

DAILY DEVOTIONAL: DAY 15

Wanting Someone Else's Life

Have you ever witnessed the success of your neighbor, co-worker, family member, or friends and felt jealousy? At times, when we look at our own lives through the lens of others' successes, we can be at risk of feeling defeated, which can lead to us believing that others are better than us. These thoughts can foster self-doubt, stir up feelings that make you wonder why you haven't prospered. You're working so hard and can't seem to meet your own needs. Many times, these thoughts can lead to bitterness, envy, and regret, creating problems for our own sense of peace and ability to champion all of God's blessings. Proverbs 23:7 (KJV) says this, "For as he thinketh in his heart, so is he." When we allow ourselves to operate in envy, jealousy, and bitterness, this is who we become. We have to remember that God has a unique plan for each of our lives and not allow that envy to control who we become.

Isaac, the firstborn son of Abraham and Sarah, married a woman named Rebekah, and, from this union, twins were conceived. The Lord said to Rebekah that two nations were in her womb, and the separation of two peoples had begun in her body; the one people shall be stronger than the other, and the elder shall serve the younger. When her days to be delivered were fulfilled, behold, there were twins in her womb. The first came out red all over like a hairy garment, and they named him Esau (hairy). Afterward, his brother came forth, and his hand grasped Esau's heel, so he was named Jacob (supplanter). Both brothers were deeply loved by their parents. But the love they had for both was divided. Abraham loved Isaac and Rebekah loved Esau, thus creating envy and jealousy between them both. After a long day of work, Isaac entered the home where he found his brother Esau cooking, and he was hungry. He asked his brother to give him something to eat. Esau, with jealousy in his heart in that he knew that Isaac was loved more than he by their father, exposed his plot whispered in his ear by Rebekah, his mother. He said that he would give him food if he gave him his birthright. Isaac, being the eldest, would receive the blessing of his dad, a common custom during that time. Isaac was famished, and, at that moment, he didn't care what his brother asked for. He agreed. His brother and mother's plan worked. Esau completed his plot by deceiving his blind father Abraham by putting on animal hair all over his body and presented himself to his father. His father could only tell it was Isaac by the hair and smell. So the blessing was given to Esau, leaving Isaac with resentment, anger, and bitterness. These brothers waged war against one another for years. But, God's hand is always upon us, working on our behalf. He makes our resentment and envy against one another transform into forgiveness, and His purpose triumphs in our lives. Read the book of Genesis starting at chapter 25.

Reflection

Think of a time where bitterness, jealousy, or envy ruled your thoughts. After identifying a time, reflect on how God still provided for you during that time.

_____

_____

_____

_____

_____

_____

_____

Are there other areas in your life that you do not trust God and prefer that He not intervene? Be honest. Remember, the goal is to allow God to renew our minds and conform our will to His will. Write down your thoughts below.

_____

_____

_____

_____

_____

_____

_____

Prayer

Lord, I know You have great plans for my life. Help me to see Your plan with clarity. You said in Your Word that we have not because we ask not. Lord, I ask for wisdom and understanding. I desire to think more like Jesus. Show me how to make great decisions and how to not allow bitterness, envy, or jealousy rule my heart. Forgive me for times where I have, and thank You for continuing to meet my daily needs even in the midst of those times. I trust Your provision for my life and the lives of my family at all times. In Jesus' name. Amen.

DAILY DEVOTIONAL: DAY 16

Leaning on The Lord When Impatience and Anxiety Consume You

My day started off great; I was offering up praise and worship to the Lord and felt a sense of calm. I had a few errands to run, yet I was grateful that I was even able to do this. Then, I got home, checked the mail, and received a correspondence that required my immediate attention. As my husband and I made our way to the bank, I started to feel anxious to resolve this issue quickly. Walking up to the teller, I began explaining what I needed to take care of. She seemed to not fully understand what I needed, which required her to make several phone calls for assistance. When she hung up the phone, she attempted to instruct me on what was needed on my end to resolve the issue, yet as she was explaining, I felt unsure about the information being given, and my confidence in her continued to reduce. I could feel myself becoming anxious. While she got back on the phone, I decided to pray, saying, "Lord, You said in Your word to 'be anxious for nothing but in everything by prayer and supplication, with thanksgiving, let your request be made known to God; and the peace of God, which surpasses all understanding, guard your hearts and minds through Christ Jesus'" (Philippians 4:6-8, NKJV). Yet as the transaction continued, it seemingly became even more complicated, which furthered my anxiety and, now, frustration. However,

I continued to say the scripture and practice patience. Once I decided to demonstrate the scripture, not just recite it, I recognized that my attitude changed regarding the situation, which caused me to humble myself before the Lord—and before the woman helping me—and allow the calmness of God to take over.

In retrospect, I realize that, no matter how anxious I became, the representative remained calm, kind, and helpful. It was important for God to remind me of her kindness and patience because I must remember to remain humble and that it is God who gives us the strength needed to take a deep breath when life's moments of anxiety and stress may overtake us.

Reflection

Below, write down a moment when anxiousness or impatience overwhelmed you. Once you've got an example, write down how God was able to remind you of His peace that surpasses all understanding and how to practice humility within the situation.

_____

_____

_____

_____

_____

_____

_____

_____

Prayer

Lord, thank You for showing me how to walk humbly before You. Help me walk in the fruit of the spirit with others in love, joy, peace, patience, kindness, goodness, faithfulness, gentleness, and self-control. I pray for temperance when dealing with challenging situations. In Jesus' name. Amen.

DAILY DEVOTIONAL: DAY 17

When Your Past Tries to Define You

For I know the thoughts that I think toward you, says the Lord, thoughts of
peace and not of evil, to give you a future
and a hope.

Jeremiah 29:11 (NKJV)

Has anyone ever said, "I know you. You are that same person that cheats, steals, drinks, and causes chaos and is no good." However, you know that God has transformed you into a new creature in Christ Jesus. So often, we try to demonstrate our newness in Jesus, but the people we know will not accept our change. They bring up old behaviors and continue to hold us accountable for the pain and suffering we may have caused them.

When I was younger, during the summers, my family and I would visit my aunt in Houston, Texas. During our vacation, we barbecued, attended church, played card games, and talked all night. Our gatherings included other family members that lived in the area as well. Our cousins and I would walk up and down the neighborhood laughing and reminiscing about the fun we had when they visited California. During family time, laughter and singing, I would go into my aunt's bedroom and find my way to her jewelry box, helping myself to a ring or bracelet. Admittedly, I was stealing; I was a thief. Soon our family vacation would come to an end, and we'd travel back to California. Me with my new ring. One day after arriving in California, my aunt called and asked to speak with me; she said, "I know you have been stealing my jewelry, and you will stop." I felt embarrassed, guilty, and ashamed.

In retrospect, my aunt was declaring that I would not be a thief. She knew the plans for my life did not include stealing. God knows the thoughts He has for us, saith the Lord, thoughts of good and not of evil, to give us a future of hope. God believes in us even when we and others don't.

"Therefore if anyone is in Christ, he is a new creation. The old has passed away. Behold, the new has come" (2 Corinthians 5:17). We are no longer defined by our past. God has called us according to His purpose. Walk boldly in the things of God.

Reflection

Write down how God has transformed your life. Reflect on the new you. What areas in your life need transforming?

_____

_____

_____

_____

_____

_____

_____

_____

_____

Prayer

Lord, thank You. I am a new creature in You, and my past does not define me. I embrace the new beginnings in my life directed by You. I receive Your love with open arms. Thank You for meeting me right where I was. You know every hair on my head, and I trust You with my life. In Jesus' name, I pray. Amen.

DAILY DEVOTIONAL: DAY 18

When the Weight of Adversity Seems to Overtake Us

The highway of the upright is to depart from evil: he that keepeth his way preserveth his soul.

Proverbs 16:17 (KJV)

Reading the verse above, I am reminded of Saul on his road to Damascus. In Acts 9, Saul received marching orders from the Jewish Sanhedrin's to go and arrest Christians, Jews, and anyone that preached in the name of Jesus. Following those directions, Saul led some of the most violent acts of persecution against Christians. Yet, something happened on the road to Damascus—a supernatural encounter with the Lord Jesus.

Just before reaching Damascus, the Lord shone a light on Saul, and he fell to his knees, blinded. Jesus asked him, "Why thou persecute me, Saul?" Saul was shaken and ashamed, realizing that what he had been doing was wrong. After Saul recognized his wrongdoing, Jesus gave him specific instructions that included where he would go and whom he would see and, in a representation of God's grace, Jesus forgave Saul for what he had done. Jesus changed Saul's wicked ways into good ways that served him. And God continued to bless Saul, giving him back his sight through the spoken word of healing spoken by the priest Ananias. God's grace and mercies.

Just as God showed grace towards Saul, God shows grace through His love towards us. He transforms us into the people we are called to be, no matter how bad the situation may look. God is faithful to forgive us of all our unrighteousness and place us in right standing with Him. God wants us to experience His sovereignty and loving kindness in our sinful state, as He did with Saul. The will of God is that no man perishes and that all men be saved from darkness by drawing us to His marvelous light. Just as He did with Saul, who was made new when Jesus changed his name to Paul—a name that represented newness through Christ Jesus; a newness that is available to us through the acceptance of His salvation.

Reflection

Imagine laying down the weight of the world, family, marriage, work, and illness. How would you respond to Jesus when He calls your name? If Jesus were to stop you on the road to Damascus, would you hear and respond to His voice? Write down areas in your life where you have not responded to the voice of Jesus. What areas of your life need the intervention of Jesus?

_____

_____

_____

_____

_____

_____

_____

_____

Prayer

Lord, thank You for loving us unconditionally and leading us through the valley. Lord, I need Your intervention in my life. When I feel weak and unsure of my relationship with You, please call my name because I recognize that You are all I need in my life. Thank You for making the crooked road straight. I pray for the renewing of my mind. In Jesus' name, I pray. Amen.

DAILY DEVOTIONAL: DAY 19

Lord, I Am Exhausted and Can't Seem to Find My Way

> For he that is entered into his rest, he also
> has ceased from his own work as God did
> from his.
>
> **Hebrews 4:10 (KJV)**

I once worked for a company where the demands of each day began to wear my body down. I found myself in a state of exhaustion, making it difficult to prepare for work, as my body seemed weaker day after day. The weekends would come, but I couldn't find the energy to get the shopping, cleaning, and caring for my family done. I was neglecting myself and everything else that was around me. And just like my story, there were so many in the Bible who experienced this kind of exhaustion as well.

In the book of Exodus, chapter 17 (KJV), Moses' hands became tired. It is noted that when Moses' hands were up high, the children of Israel prevailed, and when his hands were lowered, they were defeated. His brothers, Aaron and Hur, would hold up his hands when he was tired so that the Israelites would prevail. Imagine the burden carried and pressure felt by Moses carrying and leading the Israelites.

And just like Moses had hit his limits from time to

time, we experience exhaustion and become fatigued as caregivers, parents, teachers, friends, or employees. In these moments, one of the greatest realizations I had, specifically when reflecting on the story of Moses and his brothers, is the importance of us allowing our family and close friends to help. Moses had to acknowledge and accept that he needed help to coordinate, organize, and lead the people, eventually delegating and assigning leaders to be in charge of tribes. Once he opened his heart to help, God was able to provide for the needs of His people, and this allowed Moses to rest.

> And, on the seventh day, God ended his work which he had made; and he rested on the seventh day from all his work which he had made.
>
> Genesis 2:2 (KJV)

It's important to remember that God is concerned about our well-being and balance. God created a day of rest for Himself to show us that we should take the time to rest as well. Start today by creating a day where you enter into God's rest. It is important to lay in the presence of God. There He will restore, recover, rejuvenate, and reset your body, heart, mind, and spirit.

Reflection

Write down how to plan to enter into God's rest. What strategies will you commit to in planning time to rest with God?

_____

_____

_____

_____

_____

_____

_____

Prayer

Today, Lord, I choose to enter into Your peaceful rest. I lay every burden down and lie before You in silence. Thank You for restoring, reviving, rejuvenating my body, mind, and spirit. I turn my heart to Yours and receive balance in my life. In Jesus' name. Amen.

DAILY DEVOTIONAL: DAY 20

The Seed Within a Seed

Early Saturday morning is my dedicated time with the Lord, finding a quiet place to have a conversation with God. On Saturday morning, while spending my time giving thanks and worshipping in His presence, I noticed that God had placed upon my heart a desire for gardening. Finding myself inspired and excited by this newness, I went to the store and purchased a mango the following week. Once I got home, I began to peel the orange, yellow, and red-tinted skin off, and beneath the skin was this nice yellow meat filled with sweet juice. As I continued to eat the mango, getting closer to its center, I noticed a hard pit, which piqued my curiosity. Wanting to know more, I took it a little further and opened up the pit, only to find a smooth white seed covered by a clear sheath. Immediately, I thought about our physical body as the shell, spirit as the sheath, and the actual seed protected by the sheath as our soul. As I continued to ponder this, I began to see how important it is to understand our soul prospering. The word of God saturates our spirit, which nourishes our soul. If we are spiritually depraved, then our soul is affected, yet if we are spiritually sound, then our soul will prosper.

Beloved, I wish above all things that thou
mayest prosper and be in health, even as
thy soul prospereth.

3 John 1:2 (KJV)

The seed that I opened represented the soul. If I opened a seed that was dry, cracked, and brittle, it is unhealthy, yet if it is moist, whole, and strong, it is well. The word of God says to be in good health, and our souls will prosper. Watering our souls daily with the word of God will maintain our healing, strength, faith, and keep us well.

Reflection

Take a moment to examine yourself. Sit at the table with Jesus, have a conversation with Him regarding the state of your spirit, mind, and body. Are you in a healthy or unhealthy state? What strategies will you implement so that your soul continues to prosper and you are in good health?

_____

_____

_____

_____

_____

_____

_____

Prayer

Thank You, Lord, for sowing seeds of love in my heart and for pruning me when I am broken. The Holy Spirit reminds me of what I have heard and was taught about the love of Jesus. Let me be an example of the care that Jesus has for me to others. Hide me in the shadow of Your wings when life seems overwhelming. Cause me to have courage to know when I have disconnected from You so that I may repent and reconnect to Your goodness. Water my faith daily, reminding me that, even with the faith of a mustard seed, I can move mountains. Lord, in Your mercy, hear my prayers.

DAILY DEVOTIONAL: DAY 21

When Your Heart's Desires Don't Align up With the Will of God

Commit to the Lord whatever you do, and
he will establish your plans.

Proverbs 16:3 (NIV)

It was a very busy family day. There were chores to be done, grocery shopping, and preparing meals for a family of five. My husband and I decided to grocery shop first. Our boys, at the time, were young and loved to go grocery shopping. When I would leave the cart in the care of my husband, our sons would fill the cart with their favorite treats. Of course, the food items they chose were not on the grocery list. So, it went back on the shelves—though I admit, sometimes, they did convince me to buy a few of their favorite things. Arriving home later that afternoon, I began to feel overwhelmed emotionally and started to cry. My husband asked me, "Why are you crying?" I said, "Why did I not have any girls? God has given us all these boys, and I wanted girls too. I don't have a daughter to comb her hair or go shopping with. I wanted to experience her first boyfriend, be a part of her wedding planning and hold her first baby." My emotions grew stronger. "I've always felt with boys that they grow up, go off with their girlfriends, marry, and spend all their time with their wives' families.

I even thought I would hardly ever see any of my future grandchildren. I really wanted girls too and wish God had given us one." The thoughts I had in my head created frustration, and I was angry with God, even blaming God for our sons not being available to care for my husband and me when we grow old. What selfish thoughts; everything was about me. I never considered God's perfect plan for my three sons' lives. I love my boys deeply, but I felt it was unfair that I was the only woman in the family surrounded by all these men. At the time, I was in my early thirties. I am now in my sixties and, a few days ago, I heard the Lord say, "Daughter, I have given you these boys so you may begin to love men again." I cried after hearing these words. God was right. I had been so traumatized by my first husband, who physically and mentally abused me, and the molestation by men I had experienced at such a young age that I feared men and did not trust them. I did not realize how deeply rooted these painful events in my life were. Yet, God knew. He reminded me of His love and why He surrounded me with three wonderful sons and my amazing husband. Their hearts were filled with the love of God, and that makes me happy.

When I reflect on the love of God in my life, I see that God provided me with sons that are my rear guard, front guard, and two side guards. The guard was a reflection of His love for me through our sons. I shared what God revealed to me with my husband, and he said tenderly, "You were supposed to have boys, and through our sons, God showed you how to love men again without any hindrance." God is faithful, even when we are not. He loves even when we can not love, and He forgives when we are unable to forgive. He shows us how to forgive ourselves and others with His help. And through the love that God showed through my three sons, I was able to forgive the men that traumatized my life, yet most of all, I was able to forgive myself. God's perfect plan.

Reflection

Identify three challenges in your life that caused you to question God's plan for your life. How did it make you feel? Choose a scripture to help you reconnect to the loving plan God has for your life. After reflecting below, write your scripture down on an index card or piece of paper and tape it to your mirror or in an area to remind you of the love of God.

_____

_____

_____

_____

_____

_____

_____

_____

Prayer

"Lord, search me, and know my heart; test me and know my anxious thoughts. See if there is any offensive way in me, and lead me in the way of everlasting" (Psalm 129:23-24, NIV). In Jesus' name. Amen.

DAILY DEVOTIONAL: DAY 22

What Defers Hope?

I remember when I enrolled in a Masters of Nursing program online. I worked full time, and, to say the least, it was a challenge balancing work, family, and school. My days and nights were long, and by the end of each day, I was exhausted.

One of the assignments included a group project. We completed the project and submitted it for grading. After we received our graded assignment back, we were informed by the professor that one of the students' portions was plagiarised. Our group was devastated. We submitted a grievous and requested an upper-level review, and, thankfully, the review was granted, and the student resubmitted her paper. Along with this moment of what felt like defeat, I worked even harder to complete the requirements of the master program, yet unfortunately received a "C"; to pass the course, it required at least a "B." Yet grace was given, and I was allowed to repeat the class portion and resubmit the assignment, but only managed to receive a "C+." The instructor contacted me and said, "I know how hard you worked on the paper, but it was not master quality." I was devastated. I felt like my efforts were in vain. At least that was my thinking.

My exhaustion had gotten the best of me, and my tears would not stop flowing. I decided to take some time to grieve this loss, for, while I completed the program, due to my "C+," I did not receive my nursing master's. It still haunts me at times today. I felt hopeless, and I had failed at the very craft that I had been practicing for over forty-four years. It began to feel as if my journey as a nurse halted. But then I was reminded of my journey as a registered nurse and recalled all of the wonderful accomplishments along the way, excellent patient care, moments of educating new graduates, and supporting new employees as they entered into the field. I decided to fix my eye on my contributions, and that was when I began to find a sense of peace.

I was not hopeless. Though I did not receive the actual paper stating Masters of Nursing, the courses strengthened my leadership skills, sharpened my ability to assess, evaluate, and develop processes that improve the quality of care for patients. And God was still God; I had to cast down the thought of failing and replace it with the hope and trust that God provides—the same God who called me to nursing.

"May the God of hope fill you with all joy and peace in believing, so that by the power of the Holy Spirit you may abound in hope" (Romans 15:15, ESV). I was comforted by this scripture.

Reflection

Write down an area in your life where hope has been deferred. How did God restore your hope and cause you to feel valued again?

_____

_____

_____

_____

_____

_____

_____

_____

Prayer

Lord, I have hope in my future because it was and is created by You. You have everything I need to perform here on Earth. Thank You for every gift and skill. Thank You for Your wisdom and understanding and for surrounding me with loving people that cheer me on when I feel defeated. Help me to always remember to glorify You in all that I do. In Jesus' name. Amen.

DAILY DEVOTIONAL: DAY 23

I Am the Vine

On New Year's Day, January 2021, I decided to prune my tomato vines. While pruning, I heard the Lord say, "Gentle with pruning. Never cut the vine; it is the source of nutrients." It was a reminder that the vines are the source of life for these plants; the vine is the sustainer of the fruit while dead branches and leaves hinder the growth of new fruit. As I continued to cut the dead leaves, I found myself becoming impatient with the process. The vines were twisted and curled, leaves were dry, and some withered, making it difficult to prune. As I continued, the Lord said, "It's painful to be pruned back; it's the time to be gentle and tender through the process as I am gentle and tender in removing dead things in your life that hinder your growth in me." He began to instruct me to lay each branch gently over the gate, protecting them from damage; I discovered that beneath all the dry, dead leaves, there were beautiful tomatoes hidden and tangled.

> I am the vine, ye are the branches: He that abideth in me, and In his, the same bringeth forth much fruit: for without me ye can do nothing.
>
> **John 15:5 (KJV)**

We, as the tomatoes, must bear good fruit. In order to do this, we must understand our lives are nothing without Jesus, who is the vine. We must accept the pruning; the process may seem difficult and painful, yet the gentleness and tenderness of Jesus will refine and reshape us until we bear fruit. Amen.

> Every branch in me that beareth not fruit he taketh away: and every branch that beareth fruit, he purgeth it, that it may bring forth more fruit.
>
> **John 15:2 (KJV)**

Reflection

Write down a time where the process was hard and difficult—a time when there was need for pruning in your life.

_____

_____

_____

_____

How did God transform your withered fruit into fresh, overflowing fruit?

_____

_____

_____

_____

Day 23

Prayer

Thank You, Lord, that I abide in You, and You abide in me. Without You, I am unable to bear good fruit. I depend on Your pruning and purging. Thank You that I am already cleansed by the word of God. Help me not to get twisted and tangled by fruit vines that are not of You. I receive Your gentle, tender mercies in my life and am nurtured by Your word. In Jesus' name, I pray. Amen.

DAILY DEVOTIONAL: DAY 24

Navigating Sadness

It is the year 2021, and over the last few days, I have thought about ways to be grateful in times that seem to be filled with chaos, sadness, division, and uncertainty. These thoughts and questions have weighed heavy on my heart. With all the noise around us, how can we think of being grateful?

> When the righteous cry for help, the Lord hears and delivers them out of all their trouble. The Lord is near to the broken-hearted and saves the crushed in spirit.
> **Psalm 34:17-18**

At the top of the year, my husband and I decided to search for his older brother. After numerous calls and drives sixty miles away from our home, we reached a standstill. Discouraged, we decided to terminate our search. It was hard making this decision; my husband had such a strong desire to locate his brother as their dad had just passed away, and we wanted to break the news to him.

One day my husband received a call from the executor of his dad's estate; his older brother had been killed by a hit-and-run driver. We could not believe it and did not want to accept this news. We decided to start our search again, looking for all recent accidents that occurred in the county where he lived. To our disbelief, we found the information on the accident; his full name and date of birth—killed by a hit-and-run driver. My husband, who does not cry much, began to cry uncontrollably; the tears flowed down his cheek, and sadness filled his heart. He decided to contact his six siblings to share the news. Dealing with the death of their father and now his brother's was quite challenging. Navigating through the sadness took time, comfort, and love—the love of family, friends, and, most of all, God's.

Navigating sadness is an individual process, a journey that only you and God can navigate together. The loss of a loved one is grievous, and there are many different emotions that affect us daily. My husband and I experienced shock and denial immediately; we were in disbelief. Pain and guilt hit hard, even though we attempted several times to locate him. Anger settled in, and the desire to negotiate with God for his brother to be alive overwhelmed us daily. At times the depression entered and caused us to stop functioning. But then something happened in our situation: we began to accept the truth and allow ourselves to work through the grieving process; hope began to cultivate again. It was through prayer and staying in the presence of God that helped us get through these losses. I often wonder what would my husband and I have done if we did not have each other to get through these times. I would hope that God would remain the center of our lives and help us navigate sad times in our lives with His loving kindness and tender mercies.

I'm grateful.

Reflection

How has God helped you through navigating sadness?

_____

_____

_____

_____

Prayer

Lord, we need Your presence to help us navigate sad times in our lives. You are our cornerstone, and we lean on Your wisdom and understanding. We don't see everything like You do, and at times we lose hope. Help us to always know You are there for us and that You would never leave us alone. Help us experience Your presence daily through the word of God. Guide us away from fear, and when we are dismayed, remind us that You are God. The God who strengthens, helps, and upholds us in Your righteous right hand. In Jesus' name, I pray. Amen.

DAILY DEVOTIONAL: DAY 25

Lights Out in California

During the third week of January 2021, there have been fires, heavy winds, chaos in the White House, and people dying every day from the COVID-19 pandemic. Many people are wondering where they can find peace or who they should run to for answers. I found myself asking the same question one evening when the heavy winds took over my home.

One evening, as my husband and I prepared for bed, we heard the howling winds; they were so wild and so fierce that they caused all of the windows and doors of our house to shake. Traveling at seventy miles per hour, it sounded as if there was a battle of the winds outside of our bedroom window. The trees swayed, patio items shifted from left to right, and we could feel the strength of the cold breaking in. I, admittedly, was scared and nervous about any potential damage.

When my husband and I awoke the following morning, we noticed that the electricity was off. Grabbing our cell phones, we searched for local updates, finding out that there had been rolling blackouts within our area due to the wind storm. My husband got out of bed and went to check on the water temperature, and, to our surprise, the water was still hot. We rushed and showered immediately to find relief from the previous cold night. As our morning continued, we discovered that the refrigerator was not working and that the water had been turned off quickly after we had each taken showers. We were unsure of what to do and felt stuck without a plan of action.

That evening, as electricity returned for many of the homes within the area, the homes in our neighborhood remained dark. Still feeling unsure while also understanding that all we could do was wait it out, I asked my husband to join me for intercessory prayer. We held hands, opening our hearts and minds to the Lord: "Lord, we rejoice in You even during times of trouble. During tough times we embrace Your comfort and love. You are our provider, and we have more than enough. Because of You, Lord, my husband and I know what it is to have plenty. We have learned the secret of being content in any and every situation, whether well fed or hungry, whether living in plenty or in want. Thank You for supplying all our needs. In Jesus' name, we pray."

> Then Jesus spoke to them again, saying, "I am the light of the world. He who follows Me shall not walk in darkness, but have the light of life.
> **John 8:12 (NKJV)**

Our prayer time together brought both of us peace. We were thankful to enter into the presence of the Lord together. The darkness was illuminated by the light of the Lord through our prayers. And through His mighty head, a flashlight provided by a neighbor. God always has a ram in the bush.

I will thank you, Lord, with all my heart;
I will tell of all the marvelous things you
have done. I will be filled with joy because of you. I will sing praises to your
name, O Most High.

Psalm 9:1-2 (NLT)

What a comforting word to know that Jesus is the light of the world, so even in a dark time like the wind storm, there was no need to fret because Jesus was right there with us the entire time.

Reflection

Write down three words that you associate with a dark time in your life. How did the light of Jesus guide your path and draw you out of darkness?

_____

_____

_____

_____

Prayer

Lord, thank You for being the light of the world. Your light shines in our darkness to guide us towards You. We thank You for establishing our way. Help us from stumbling in the dark through Your word. Thank You for Your provision. In Jesus' name. Amen.

DAILY DEVOTIONAL: DAY 26

Pleasant words are like a honeycomb,
sweet to the soul and healing to the bones.

Proverbs 16:24 (KJV)

The tongue has the power of life and death (Proverbs 18:21). Words are powerful. When used to empower, they are sweet as a honeycomb. But when words are used to hurt, demean, and tear down the spirit of a man, they are not pleasant or sweet, nor do they heal. Words can stimulate joy and happiness, yet they can also bring about sadness, pain, and trauma. God has given us the gift of language to glorify Him in our speaking, singing, and in the unspoken word. The question becomes, what words are coming out of your mouth? Are you a builder or a destroyer? I believe we all fall short in this area. Most of the time, our emotions direct what comes out of our mouths. I remember on January 20, 2021, the Presidential Inauguration for the 46th President and Vice President aired on national television and the world wide web. The comments were rolling so fast it was difficult to read them. But there was one comment that caught my eye. It was filled with anger and hate. The person who wrote the comment said this, "I hope that the 46th President and Vice President's family die of Alzheimer's and cancer." Wow! What venomous words to declare over someone's life. I asked myself, should I write a reply or let it go? I pondered for a moment. I continued listening to the inauguration, yet

I could not move on or be silent. In my mind, this was an opportunity to spread the love of Jesus.

I prayed that God would show me how to respond; it was important to me that what I wrote was transformative and based on the Word of God. As I prayed, the Lord reminded me of Ephesians 4:29 (NKJV), "Let no corrupt word proceed out of your mouth, but what is good for necessary edification, that it may impart grace to the hearers." It was a reminder that grace and kindness should be shown to one another, that we should edify and build up others. I placed my fingers on the keyboard and typed, *Is being angry helping the situation?* With hesitation, I pressed *enter.* Of course, the writer did not respond yet. I hoped the writer seriously thought about the comment written and changed their perspective to one of love and life, the same love and life that I have discovered through God and His grace when I have had similar thoughts.

Speaking life and encouragement even in the midst of our differences is key to tapping into and reminding yourself and others of the love of God.

> The Lord your God will change your heart and the hearts of all your descendants, so that you will love him with all your heart and soul and so you may live.
> **Deuteronomy 30:6 (NLT)**

Day 26

Reflection

What words have you used this week that edified a family member or friend? Journal your words this week and see if you have shown grace through what is said. In what area has God transformed your heart?

_____

_____

_____

_____

Prayer

Lord, help us respond to others with compassion and love. You are a God that knows our deepest thoughts and fears. Renew our minds, search our hearts and see if there is any wickedness in us. Cleanse us of all unrighteousness so we can stand before You with clean hands and a pure heart. I pray that we are tenderhearted with one another in our words, both written and verbal. Forgive us for speaking evil of one another. Lord, You love us all, and we ought to love one another. In Jesus' name. Amen.

DAILY DEVOTIONAL: DAY 27

Rejoice in Victory

But thanks be to God, which giveth us
victory through our Lord Jesus Christ.

1 Corinthians 15:57 (KJV)

When God gives us the victory, it is time to dance, praise, and shout to the Lord with joy and thanksgiving. When I look towards the higher calling of Christ Jesus, I start to see the victories in my life that God was giving me through Christ Jesus. The Lord healed me of cancer, granted me the opportunity to work in the nursing field for over forty years without deficiencies or charges against my nursing license, and has sustained my family through the multiple financial disasters I've experienced. God has shown me that love casts down all fear, even in the face of my own fears. All of this as a result of accepting Jesus as my Lord and savior. Giving my life over to God through Jesus has shown me the true definition of victory. I have the privilege to be a part of the kingdom of God and inherit the benefits of His love, grace, and mercies. I felt just like the Israelites on the first day of their exodus. They were happy, singing and rejoicing in the presence of God. Even in the midst of them falling short, their disobedience and disregard for God's plans, He still showed them and has shown me that exact same grace. I am, with gratitude, a child of the Most High God, the apple of His eye, and it is because of Jesus that I live and breathe. Victory is mine because God gave it to me through the love of Jesus.

Reflection

Write down three victories God has given you this week. Write down affirmations of who you are in Christ Jesus.

_____

_____

_____

_____

_____

Through your victories written down above, take some time to identify who you are through Christ Jesus.

_____

_____

_____

_____

Prayer

Lord God, thank You for the victories in my life. Each one is special and dear to my heart. I affirm who You are in me, my Lord and Savior, The Holy Anointed one, and the author and finisher of my faith. You are the rock I stand on; I depend and rely only on You. Lord, You are faithful, righteous, and loving. Your grace is sufficient. Thank You for drawing me into Your marvelous light and for placing Your word into my heart. Lord, I will give You thanks and praise in all that I do for the rest of my days. In Jesus' name, I pray. Amen.

DAILY DEVOTIONAL: DAY 28

Finding God Between the Gaps in Life

Dear God, how are You today? I want to acknowledge and thank You for a clear mind. I surrender my thoughts and plans. I admit, there are days that I don't feel like You are there. I search and knock at the door but can't seem to find You. But, when I look outside my window, I see Your beautiful creation, and I am reminded how close You are to me.

I joined a 5 a.m. club in April. It was designed by a pastor friend of mine in the hope that we would learn our worth, walk in God's purpose and embrace who we are in Christ. The first two weeks were daunting, my body called for sleep, and my spirit said *get up*—what a constant battle. I was determined to attend the live group, and one morning I overslept. It was upsetting to me because I truly desired commitment to the group. So, I sent a quick text to the leader apologizing for missing that morning. She replied to me, "There is no guilt or condemnation; you are not held hostage. There are times when life happens, but the key is to get up and begin again." I was comforted by her words.

When we think about disappointing God, it causes us to feel guilty and sad. Some of us even tell ourselves that we are not worthy. But this is not of God.

One morning, the Spirit of God awakened me, and I

began to pray, and, during my prayer time, I heard the Lord say, "There are gaps in your life." I wrote down every word as He revealed the truth to me. I began to repent and accept his forgiveness. It was a calming, peaceful moment in the presence of the Lord. As I reviewed what God had given me, I read the instructions of the Lord. The Lord said, "Filter every thought through me today." *Filter*, I thought. I am imagining a water filter that cleans and clears our water of harmful elements. Just as the water is filtering the harmful elements in our water, Jesus filters thoughts that cause us to feel unworthy, rejected, unloved, and lonely. We must admit, our thoughts can overtake us, leaving behind stains of regret, but Jesus wants to help us filter all our thoughts and remind us who we are in Him.

> Finally, brothers and sisters, whatever is true, whatever is noble, whatever is right, whatever is pure, whatever is lovely, whatever is admirable-if anything is excellent or praiseworthy-think about such things.
>
> **Philippians 4:8 (NIV)**

Reflection

Take a moment and reflect on thoughts that caused you to feel unworthy, disappointment, and frustration today. What were you thinking at the moment? Identify and write down the thoughts on the first two lines below.

_____
_____
_____
_____
_____
_____
_____

Now on the two lines above this, write down the opposite of that. Then read them out loud, saying "*I am*" before each word. Finally, cross out each word on the first two lines as an acknowledgment that that is no longer who you are in Christ.

Prayer

Lord, You know the thoughts You have for us, thoughts of good and not of evil, of hope with an expected end. Help us to trust Your filtering system. Sift out thoughts that don't align with Your will for our lives. Teach us to rely on You completely. Guide our free will and reveal to us quickly when we have embraced thoughts that are not of You. In Jesus' name, I pray. Amen.

DAILY DEVOTIONAL: DAY 29

The Essence of Forgiveness

Unforgiveness can be a stronghold, choking the very life out of us if we are not careful to cancel the debt of wrongdoing to us by others. I'd mentioned earlier in this devotion book of my experience with molestation, and, had it not been for the Lord on my side, I would not have chosen to forgive my assailant. But, with God, all things are possible, even a forgiving heart.

In Genesis 37, God tells us the story of Jacob and Rachel's youngest son of eleven, Joseph. He was loved dearly by his parents. His parents seemed pleased with everything he did. He was obedient, giving, and loving without conditions, always honoring both his mother and father, and all of this made his brothers jealous. One story, in particular, tells of a cloak that Rachel made his son Joseph before she passed away. After her death, during a family dinner, Jacob presented the cloak to Joseph as a reminder of how much his mother, Rachel, loved him. As the family continued dinner, Joseph shared a dream that he had the night prior; in the dream, his older siblings bowed down before him. With much dismay, the oldest son spoke up, saying, "We will not bow down to you; I'm the eldest brother. The blessing came to me." His other older brothers were also furious, laughing at him and refusing to acknowledge his dream.

As the anger and jealousy grew amongst Joseph's nine older brothers, they created a plan to kill him, deciding that they would beat him, take his cloak, pour blood from a lamp over it, tear it to shreds, and leave him there for dead. When they left Joseph there to die, little did the brothers know that the dream Joseph had was, in fact, from God.

As Joseph lay in dirt, hurt and brutalized by his brothers, a passerby who worked for the Pharaoh found him and sold him into slavery—unforgivable. While in slavery, Joseph endured many trials and suffrage from prison to deception and lies. Yet one day, at the beckoning of the Pharaoh, Joseph interpreted a dream the Pharaoh had, ensuring that no lack of food during the coming famine would impact Egypt. As a result of this interpretation coming true, the Pharaoh elevated him to the highest position outside of his vizier; Joseph was now the Governor of Egypt. His brothers, sure that he was dead, were unaware of this blessing that had been placed upon Joseph's life.

As God's plan for Joseph was in motion, a famine hit all of the other nations, including that of his father and brothers. One day, Joseph's father and brothers arrived to buy grain and wheat, unaware that Joseph was the Governor. Upon their arrival, Joseph summoned them to be brought to him. When they arrived, they did not recognize Joseph, yet once they did, they wept. Joseph, granted the grace of mercy of God, forgave his brothers for the wrongdoing, kissing them each individually and asking that they also forgive themselves. He then blessed them, and the Pharaoh provided them with everything that they needed.

Be Kind and compassionate to one another, forgiving each other, just as in Christ
God forgave you.

Ephesians 4:32 (NIV)

We must remember that forgiving ourselves and others opens the heart of God. Just as Jesus died on the cross for us for the remission of our sins and pardoned us, we must also forgive those who have wronged us. Forgiveness is a choice. Unforgiveness is a sin. It binds up and gives life to dark areas that separate us from God. We must be willing to invite God into our unforgiving hearts through our confession and repentance.

Reflection

Why do you think forgiveness is important?

_____

_____

_____

_____

_____

Now, identify three ways unforgiveness has affected your life and how you'd like to see God help you in your process of forgiveness.

_____

_____

_____

Prayer

Lord, help us release unforgiving thoughts that hinder us from living a full life in Christ. We embrace the essence of forgiveness and refuse to give place to the enemy. I confess that I have been living an unforgiving life, mad at the world for all the wrongdoings that I have allowed to affect my life. God, I confess that I have been mad with You as well. Today I come to You asking for forgiveness for the thoughts that have held my heart and mind hostage. Teach me to forgive quickly so that I may release others into Your forgiving hand; teach me not to keep track of wrongdoing and embrace the spirit of forgiveness that Joseph had. In Jesus' name, I pray. Amen.

DAILY DEVOTIONAL: DAY 30

Opening Your Heart Today to Receive Jesus as Your Lord and Savior

I never want to miss the opportunity of anyone wanting to receive Jesus. "If we confess our sins, He is faithful and just to forgive us our sins and to cleanse us from all unrighteousness" (1 John 1:9, KJV). God has opened the door through Jesus to come just as we are. He has no respect for people, meaning He does not judge you for what you have been doing, but He is pleased when you have chosen to accept Him into your heart by faith.

In John 3, we hear about the story of Nicodemus, the ruler of the Jews. While speaking to Jesus in the still of the night, he inquired about the concept of being reborn again as he could not understand how one could return to his mother's womb. Jesus tells Nicodemus that unless one is born again, he cannot see the kingdom of God, saying, "Most assuredly, I say to you, unless one is born of water and the Spirit, he cannot enter the kingdom of God" (John 3:1-7, KJV).

Through this verse, God is inviting us to be reborn, and we are able to experience this through the Lord Jesus Christ. If you are ready to give your life over to Jesus today, please read this prayer knowing that I am praying it with you: "Lord, I come to You as I am with an open heart to receive You today. I ask for forgiveness for the things I have done over the course of my life. I surrender to You. I believe by faith that Jesus is the son of God and was raised from the dead. Come into my heart and be the Lord over my life. Amen."

If you have said this simple prayer, welcome to the kingdom of God. I pray you join a local church in your area that accepts all people and preaches the true gospel of Jesus Christ.

> For God so loved the world, that he gave his only begotten Son, that whosoever believeth in him should not perish, but have everlasting life.
>
> **John 3:16 (KJV)**

God bless you. I pray that this devotion has drawn you closer to Jesus and blessed you beyond measure.

CPSIA information can be obtained
at www.ICGtesting.com
Printed in the USA
BVHW040253260122
627128BV00010B/863